Islands Apart

£7

Tw

19/2/

(3)

To Barbara and George

Islands Apart
The Isles of Scilly

Eighty Monochrome Plates
and Text by

John Hunt

WRUFF
PUBLICATIONS

1989

Published in Great Britain by
Wruff Publications,
Porthloo, St Mary's,
Isles of Scilly.

FIRST EDITION 1989

Book Design by 41 Design,
Dorchester, Dorset.

Printed in Great Britain by
Henry Ling Limited
(The Dorset Press),
Dorchester, Dorset.

British Library Cataloguing in Publication Data
Hunt, John
Islands Apart: The Isles of Scilly.
1. Isles of Scilly. Description & Travel.
1. Title
914. 23' 790858

Case Bound ISBN 1 872156 00 2
Soft Bound ISBN 1 872156 01 0

Preface

Here is another book about the Isles of Scilly. A book to be looked at, read, enjoyed and experienced by all lovers of Scilly. This book, like the islands themselves, has something for almost everyone.

John Hunt has produced many interesting and original thoughts and observations which, with the varied collection of photographs, offer new and different perspectives of the islands.

Anyone, like myself, who has worked as a flower picker will empathise with his comments on the subject, as will someone who has failed to puchase an elusive Turk's Head pasty.

Like many, John has found Scilly a place to be enjoyed either alone or with company. He obviously gains pleasure roaming all around the islands, but with his eyes wide open and lens cap off.

Whilst it may appear that the author spends most of his time drifting around eating and drinking, he is an intriguing character and it seems that every step, each photograph and every swig of beer is carefully thought out and, above all, experienced and enjoyed. His text is not cluttered with details but is interestingly thought out, like the composition of each photograph.

John Hunt has captured in words and superb photography some of the atmosphere of the Isles and has managed to portray something of their unique magic and mystery, which seems to hold some of us here and persuades many to return...again and again.

Roy Duncan.
Chairman for the Council of
the Isles of Scilly.

Plate 1

Introduction

If you are looking for an in-depth guide book with a ten-page index full of historical names and events then I sincerely advise you to put this book back on the shelf. This is a book of impressions. My impressions. Living in a place like Scilly, one cannot help but have strong feelings and thoughts about these small, remote islands. I was not born here, and do not claim to be Scillonian: but Scilly is in my heart. I breathe its air, drink its water and move with its moods.

Islands are my adopted habitat. Being born and bred in London, I suppose it is not too surprising that I should have reacted to extreme, preferring the tangibility of small islands to the alienation of inner-city life, where proportions pay no heed to the human scale of things.

Through my work as a photographer, I have visited many off-shore islands, always returning to London like a fledgling to its nest until one groggy morning I left for good, leaving London and not stopping till I made Penzance and then on, a further forty miles to the Isles of Scilly.

Chapter One

A question in a recent competition asked 'How many islands make up the Isles of Scilly?' One book says just over fifty while another states that there are over one hundred: opinions vary. First you have to decide at what point an island becomes a rock. The best definition I think is, if it can support one sheep for one year then it is an island. Without actually commandeering some poor unfortunate sheep, I would say there were about forty true islands, but it is still only a guess. Of those forty islands only six are inhabited by Man.

All the islands are small. The total area of Scilly is only four thousand acres: that's about two acres per islander. The islands are like samples, the results of an apprentice perfecting his geological skills before going on to attempt something a little more adventurous, like Britain or Ireland. St Mary's is the largest of the inhabited islands followed by Tresco, St Martin's, St Agnes, Bryher and the smallest, Gugh.

In the following pages I have not made much mention of St Mary's: most of the plates, however, were taken on the island. I live and work on St Mary's; it is my adopted home. The majority of people who visit Scilly have to land on St Mary's at least once, and most of the visitors make the island their base.

St Mary's is like a sieve, collecting all the input, retaining most of it and filtering the rest out to the off-islands. It's the stop gap. If St Mary's is a world away from the mainland, then the off-islands are twice removed.

Transport to the off-islands is limited during the winter. In the summer, the launches ferry people back and forth, cutting through the clear water with the excitement of a school outing. Throughout the winter, the launches convalesce at the Porthloo boatyard. Out of the water, they are massive, looming objects. On a windy December day, sand twirls and spins and the yard takes on the lonely aspect of an elephant's graveyard. By the arrival of March, the boats have been overhauled, rubbed down and repainted to a glossy glory. All have their own colours and all have their own skippers. Large blackboards with chalk-written tables show which launch is going to which island. Every day, the launches swap destination so it is possible to stick with the same launch and do all the different trips; to Bryher and Samson, Tresco, St. Martin's, the Eastern Isles, St. Agnes and Gugh, the Norrard Rocks and, of course, the 'See the Seals' trip around the Bishop Rock Lighthouse and the Western Rocks.

The Eastern Isles are a wonderful collection of pocket-sized islands. The first time I was taken around them on a launch, it was all too confusing. The sun was making our boatload of trippers lazy, too lazy to work out whether it was Great or Little Arthur which was on our port side and too overwhelmed to realise that the seal which the skipper had just pointed out was in fact Seal Rock, a cunningly shaped lump of granite on Great Ganilly. I did realise one thing on that trip: I wanted to return, to ramble over those heathery tops and look about me at this clutch of gentle, green worlds.

I did not have to wait too long to fulfil my desire. A week later, a new friend took me to Nornour. She sat on top of the four-acre island gazing at St Martin's while I pushed my way through the thick fern and bracken. Holding my cameras in the air away from the seasoned cobwebs, I circled Nornour. The tide was against us, and too soon she signalled that we should go.

We chugged peacefully around Nornour's larger companions. The light was fading, the sea birds were silent. On our right, a seal broke the silky surface of the water, sending out a thick, slow ripple.

The islands were growing familiar. I knew Great Ganilly and Great and Little Innisvouls. On our left, a canine tooth of an island, Hanjague, stood guard over Scilly's eastern approach. The ebbing tide slowly revealed the network of connecting sandbars between the two Arthurs and the two Ganinicks.

We could have gone anywhere after that; across to St Martin's and the Seven Stones pub, to Tresco's New Inn, the Hell Bay Hotel on Bryher or even, at a stretch, the Turk's Head on St Agnes. Noises travel on nights like those. The dugh-a-dugh of an outboard motor glides across the water the way you would think the boat were just behind you. There is a drama of anticipation when something as volatile as the Atlantic Ocean becalms itself; and that evening it had laid itself open like a perfumed gown.

Since then, I have been to Great Ganilly. I have stood on Seal Rock and gazed down its sheer drop to the forest of heather a hundred feet below. Since then, I have been to many of the Scillonian islands. Yet I must admit that the wonderful proportions of Great Ganilly, its sandy East Porth, its two hills and bisecting valley and sweeping views of Scillonia have made it my favourite amongst the uninhabited isles.

To say which of the inhabited islands is my favourite would make me out to be unfaithful. They all have their own charms, and I visit them (not as often as I would like) as a man would visit his secret lovers, not saying anything of one while in the company of another. I am not as faithful to Tresco as perhaps I should be. There is an atmosphere of 'non-island', as if it were the alien of the archipelago. Maybe it is due to the fact that it is a private island and there is a landing charge. Tresco has its own advertisement in the Scillonian magazine. After reading all the various attractions the island holds, like its "three castles to explore", its "small, interesting church" and its "time share properties to buy", I get the feeling that I'm being invited by some stuffy old duffer to enter his loft and admire his extensive train set.

Yet there is no getting away from the fact that Tresco is beautiful. When I first walked through Abbey Wood on the south side of Tresco, the sun was pushing through the high branches, dripping its golden light down the cracked bark of the pines. A musty smell of damp leaves and drying needles filled my nose. Through the gaps in the trees at the foot of the hill, the long blue shock of the Great Pool lay waiting. The Great Pool nearly splits the island in two and on either side lies hillside woodland. No other Scillonian island can offer such a walk.

In bleak contrast to the lushness of Tresco is its neighbouring island, Bryher. The terrain is rough and ready. Optimum use is made of the modest area of arable land. Bryher gives the impression of a grotesque face with a goatee beard and bobble night cap, wildly scorning the Norrard rocks and the western approaches. The facial features of the western seaboard are indeed very rough. The names that the coastline holds are just about as subtle as the pounding waves that hit them - the chin of Stony Porth, the nostrils of Stinking Porth and the large dent in the night cap of the notorious Hell Bay. House of the Head on Shipman Head (which would be the 'bobble') is also a name to conjure with. Somehow, Droppy Nose Point doesn't quite fit in with the scheme of things, but as a name it is quirky and delightful. The town is spread along the east coast facing Tresco and consists of a road flanked by two strings of houses, barns and other outbuildings. The road carries on, stopping a little short of Hangman Island which suffers the indignity of being cut off at high tide on average twice a day. The same distressing inconvenience is also inflicted on Shipman Head.

On Bryher there are a couple of cafes and of course the Hell Bay Hotel, which attracts its own fair share of island-loving celebrities. At one time there was a pub called the Victory Inn: now the nearest pub is the New Inn on Tresco. The Post Office-cum-Bakery-cum-General Stores sits on the north-east side of Bryher. An inflatable rubber dinghy hangs from the Post Office sign, partly obscuring an enamelled "Fry's five boys" advertisement. Above the doorway and the Dickensian- style windows which flank it is an enamelled advert for Black Cat cigarettes. Right of the windows stands a tower of string baskets overflowing with footballs. This, then, is the height of commercialism on Bryher.

One day, I had bought a pasty from the Post Office. There was a thin veil over the sun. I walked up the rutted lane towards town, munching away. Pastry flakes caught hold of the wind, leaving a trail to be eagerly gobbled up by small birds. Up there on my right was the large green and rocky mass of Watch Hill. I had been up there earlier in the day, taking in the not unsubstantial view. For company, I had the contemplative duo of cheese sandwiches and a bottle of beer. I could see why somebody had named it Watch Hill. If you fancy a really good watch, then this is the place.

My pasty was nearly finished. I could see a man doing something outside a large shed. He was making a marker buoy. The front of the shed was covered in brushstrokes of many colours like an impressionist painting. "This will go about two miles out to sea." It was Leonard Jenkins, highly knowledgeable on all aspects of the island. He disappeared into his garage-sized shed and started to have a good rummage. By the looks of things, the collection of bits and pieces which either hung, lay or stood had taken many years to gather. "Some of this stuff belonged to my grandfather." He produced a long pole of bamboo and stepped out into the weak sunlight. "I'm going to get rid of some of it." He pointed vaguely to a pile in the corner, yet somehow I reckon it sits there still.

To look into Leonard's shed is to see how someone on Bryher needs to have the knowledge to turn his hand to many a job. It had everything from propellor blades and netting to wiring, rubber roofing and sacks of seed potatoes. Outside, his little dog, aptly named Tiny, sat at the end of a plank which served as a bench. Leonard pulled out a knife which was jabbed into the door and got to work on the bamboo. Tiny climbed up and sat on Leonard's lap, banged his furry tail against his tired, Guernsey jumper and watched the splinters of bamboo fly from his knife. Leonard's peak cap was splattered with white paint. The creases on his face said he was an old man, yet to say he was old, even on the last day of his sixty-ninth year, would be unfair.

"Have you ever been to London, Leonard?"

"Oh, I've been to London. Went up there for a big fisheries meeting. I'd rather live on an island all by myself than live in London."

There are a lot of Jenkinses on Bryher. They are supposed to have come from Wales three hundred years ago and with a name like Jenkins, it seems logical. The churchyard on Bryher is full of Jenkinses, like a family gathering. It must be nice to know that when you die you will probably be surrounded by more family than when you were alive.

The path to the quay took me past Leonard's sleeping relatives. I stayed there a while. I could see the quay from the churchyard and after a few minutes I strolled down to meet the St Mary's launch. Unfortunately, Bryher quay is rendered impotent by low tide. The ebbing sea gradually creeps away, giving itself a respite before reengaging. When the sea and quay are not ensconced, landing takes place at Rushy Bay to the south.

As we boarded the launch back to St Mary's, a black and white football floated into sight along Tresco Sound. "Where the hell do all these balls come from?" asked the skipper. "I'm always seeing the kids come back from Bryher with footballs."

From Bryher, the launches normally stop at Samson before crossing to St Mary's. The hundred and twenty acres of Samson basically consist of two twined hills separated by a narrow waist of sandy soil. From St Mary's, Samson looks like the cleavage of a submerged woman. The thick covering of bracken and bramble makes exploration hard-going. It is best to wait until the school has had its annual picnic and all the kids have flattened it from running wild. It is an unsatisfying island, lacking conclusion. The undergrowth is imposing. Relaxing headway can only be enjoyed on the few paths. Nevertheless, the views from South Hill and the emotive shells of long-abandoned cottages are beautiful and intriguing. From South Hill, you can see practically every island in Scilly. To the south are St. Agnes and Gugh, Annet, the bird sanctuary and the Western Rocks. To the north are Bryher, the

Norrard Rocks and Tresco. St. Martin's and the Eastern Isles are in the north-east and to the south-east is St. Mary's.

Although being one hundred and twenty acres, it does lack character. It is one of those islands which is better to look at than actually explore. Indeed, Great Ganilly has more character and beauty yet has to make do with a mere twenty acres. But then, I am biased.

The cottages on Samson are tucked into the northern side of South Hill. It must have been a hard living for those people, doing their best to grow crops in the sparse, sand-covered clay soil. If the two families who lived there, the Woodcocks and the Webbers, hadn't fallen out with the Mumfords and Banfields on St Mary's, then they never would have got themselves into that situation. Apparently, the different factions got a bit shirty with each other. Liquor Webber and Dicebox Woodcock had no chance against the Mumford and Banfield mafia. They were promptly proclaimed "dangers to the community" and banished to Samson. This happened some time in the seventeenth century. Liquor and Dicebox and their descendants lasted on Samson until 1855 when they were evacuated back to St. Mary's. Nineteen of the island's men were drowned one night and it was deemed that the families could no longer support themselves. It seems that everybody shook hands and made up.

Indeed, if you are ever in Hugh Town and you want some mince meat and brown rice for your tea then "Woodcock and Mumfords" is the place to go.

Chapter Two

Where the ringing of tills and the dugh-a-dugh of small outboards fill the summer's ear the slapping of wet paintbrushes and picking of narcissi fill the winter's. The mild seasons on Scilly have seen daffodils in bloom as early as September. Picking is well underway by November and aching men walk around like question marks, slowly sitting down in pubs with their pints of beer.

Bearded men ask difficult questions like "Do you fancy doing some picking then?" It had to happen sooner or later. After buying me my third pint he caught me off-guard. I said yes.

The next morning I was up at seven and donned a pair of two-sizes-too-big black wellies which had been given to me as a vague bribe. I was not sure what I was letting myself in for or what had made me agree but even so, I got myself prepared. Eventually, me and the boots were ready. I possessed the profile of a pickaxe but with my black PVC flasher's Mac and flask of Scotch broth I was ready.

The actual reality of flower picking is a far cry from the poetic bliss that it conjures up in the mind's eye - that of lolloping around, gathering here, gathering there colourful posies of bright, sweet-smelling blooms by the banks of a sun-dappled brook. Oh, if only it were. Instead, you're faced with row upon row of tightly budded green stems with only a few timid heads poking out from the tops: long rows, short rows, dainty little miniature flowers to bloody great triffids which need two hands to pull out. As well as the physical exhaustion of eight hours' a day solid back-breaking pick pick picking, come rain, hail, wind and the person in front of you farting, there is the mental exhaustion. It must rank as one of the least creative ways of knackering yourself. For every flower picked another brain cell dies until you end up with just enough collective brain power to get yourself legless. Last season in the Mermaid I informed a fellow picker that he'd had to pick about nine hundred flowers to pay for the pint he had just drained. The creaking picker gave me a sour look and woefully ordered another pint while contemplating the pound coin in his aching palm.

Earlier that day my waterproofs were like the skin of a snare drum with a million sticks beating down on it. My hands had surrendered to an icy numbness. My face was hot with the sting of hail and my warm human soul consisted of a single thread set deep into my wretched frame. One time, a painter chap was picking in an almighty wind. Normally, you would gather enough flowers under your left arm to make a bunch of about eight inches in diameter, stick an elastic band around it and leave it in a row to be collected later. However, this bloke had got so wound up trying to pick the flowers in the wind that he just kept adding to his bunch until he could hold no more. By this time, all the other pickers had stopped and were standing in the field looking at him, wondering what the hell he was up to. On reaching the end of his row, the painter turned round, looked at everybody and with an almighty yell screamed "I hate picking flowers!", after which he heaved the bunch of flowers into the air, leaving the wind to carry them off on a journey halfway across the island. The cry was primeval and expressed the feelings of pickers everywhere.

From the comfort of a path, flower-pickers take on the appearance of grazing animals, slowly munching away at the stems in a staggered line. The clicking sound of the flowers being picked travels across the fields. When four or five pickers are working, the sound drifts towards you making you think a pool of secretaries were out there typing letters for their boss.

The short sharp days of the winter months bring with them the clear air that gives the landscape its luminous quality. These are the days I prefer for photography. For a start, to get up at the crack of dawn doesn't involve having to crawl out of bed at some ungodly hour like half past four in the morning. Somehow, rubbing hands, stamping feet and watching the vapour rise from your mouth give the morning's work an extra sense of excitement. The crispness of light on a bright winter's day picks out texture and form and slaps it in your face. The sun's low lob across the southern sky keeps the shadows long all day. Rhythms are accentuated or even rediscovered from last winter. Morning slips into evening with no mention of the midday sun, and long black dogs sit undisturbed like vultures, on shoulder-high walls.

Taking photographs on St Mary's poses the problem of eliminating the many electricity and telegraph poles. Many times I have refrained from pressing the shutter release after spying the thin black lines of the cables casually languishing across the top of the composition. There are probably more poles and cables to the square mile on St Mary's than anywhere else in the world - at least it seems that way to me when, yet again, the cables cut across the bit of sky I wish to photograph. Maybe S.W.E.B. and B.T. will read this and considerately reposition the poles in a more environmentally-conscious manner. We all live in hope...

This, however, is not a problem on the off-islands. The undisrupted views from the grassy back of some outlying island sends me into a trance where the irritations of something simple like cables and poles seem to occupy another world.

Chapter Three

St Agnes is the most southerly of the inhabited isles. Its southern isolation adds to the excitement of a visit. From St Mary's quay all the other islands (apart from Annet and the Western Rocks) are to the north. The other launches fan out to St Martin's, Tresco, the Eastern Isles, Bryher and Samson while the St Agnes boat peels off quietly to the south west, the way you would think it knew the whereabouts of long ago buried treasure. From

St Mary's, most of St Agnes is obscured from view by its low tide companion, Gugh. Gugh pretends to have a lighthouse which does, in fact, sit on St Agnes. It rises above the island, blind but well loved. Only when you reach St Agnes at its small quay at Porth Conger is the secret of its long and inconsistent love affair with Gugh revealed. Golden sands stretch across from island to island, forming the bar at low tide. Gradually, as the tide rises, their grip on each other weakens until they are cut off altogether and they are left waiting for the tide to turn.

It is said that you can get the best pasties on Scilly at the Turk's Head Free House just above Porth Conger. What better way to start a day's wanderings? On inquiring about the said pasties, I was met with "Sorry mate, none today." In my grief, I ordered a pint of Guiness and a packet of 'Scilly Nuts'. The day was hot, with the glory of a fresh breeze from the west. I went outside and sat on a bench overlooking the quay. Fat seagulls sat on hot boulders. Everywhere it was knee-caps and sunglasses. People moved around like exiled pools winners. I enjoyed my pint and my 'Scilly Nuts'. I was half expecting Ronnie Biggs to stroll up with a long glass when instead two faces which were vaguely familiar appeared on the other side of the bench: not dear old Ronnie but some people I had met on the train from London to Penzance the previous Summer. "We camp on Agnes every year," said the husband in his T- shirt and shorts. "Eleven years we've been coming here. Susan, our youngest, was only a twinkle on our first trip."

"Agnes must be very familiar to you by now," I said. "Yeah, we meet the same people every year. They come on holiday at the same time as us. It's like a little club. My workmates can't understand it. They all jet off to Spain or Greece and they can't understand why A: we don't go abroad, B: we go somewhere that's 'dead' and C: that we've been going there for the last eleven years. 'Don't worry,' said one bloke, 'you'll be able to afford a proper holiday soon.' What really gets them confused is when we say that we really do enjoy ourselves. Because we know the set-up so well, it's not long after arriving that we are nicely settled in with our tent erected, bits and pieces sorted and bacon and eggs sizzling in the pan."

Maybe it would break their idealised dream if they were to actually live on the island. "We thought about living on Bryher," announced the wife. "There was a job opportunity a few years back but we decided that we didn't fancy the idea of America being our nearest westerly neighbour."

I left the couple sitting on the bench and wandered off up the island road through Higher Town towards the General Stores at Middle Town. The logic of these island stores is wonderful. They sell all the necessities you are likely to require without the fuss and pressure of hard-nosed little shops on the mainland. Not only that but, according to the Sunday Telegraph, the St Agnes store "has an excellent range of paperbacks." It's a pity that on that particular day the range of cheeses was not as prodigious as the paperbacks but you get used to these things. The St Agnes store is the most health conscious of all the off-island stores. I particularly enjoy the Tetra Brik packets of soya dessert, chocolate flavour being my favourite. Unfortunately, I had to make do with strawberry flavour that day as the sales of chocolate ones had made an unexpected leap.

The road forks at Middle Town and the destination for both roads is Lower Town so if you are out on a quiet stroll, I suggest you dig into your pocket, pull out a coin and 'heads' left, 'tails' right.

The third in the trio of towns is called Lower Town and with Higher and Middle Towns gives St Agnes the impression of a well-balanced and contented island. The two roads meet again at Lower Town on the western side of the island from where you can stroll out along the fine beach of Periglis. Across Smith Sound to the west lies the island of Annet: fifty acres of fern and bracken smothered in bird nests. It is put out of bounds in the nesting season because of its importance in the world of ornithology. Apart from being a site of special scientific interest, Annet has also featured in a Sunday paper under the glorious headline of 'Prince Charles 'headless shocker'', the sub-title stating 'Royal Row over Devil's Isle Blood Sacrifices.' This was a rather sensationalised, soaraway account of the two hundred lesser-black-backed gulls which were found beheaded on the island. It is still uncertain why somebody did this terrible thing but it's doubtful that they were carrying out an 'ancient ritual to summon the Devil'.

That day, as I walked along Periglis beach, those two hundred seagulls were probably having the time of their lives, swooping around in circles, crying with glee, with bellies full of fish and picnic offerings from excited children.

"Do you like our crocodile, mister?" Two children were taking a break from their efforts and admiring their work. The vapour trail of an air liner caught the corner of my eye and I looked up: two needle streaks of white in that thick blue sky left behind by three hundred people eating roast beef and watching 'Rambo'. I looked at the kids and their sand crocodile on that empty August beach, felt the grains in between my toes and the sun on my back. It was a fine crocodile - only "What about the eyes?"

"Oh, that's no problem Mister, our Dad has gone to look for some shells."

The back of Periglis Beach rises to form a long embankment of marram grass. On the other side of the marram grass is a large field of short grass, the cricket-cum-football pitch. With the sounds of the sea on one side and the English sound of summer cricket on the other, I laid out my food and opened my bottle of beer. I remember one time having a similar picnic out on the extreme southern point of St Agnes. Again, it was August and the rocks were fit to burst with all the heat. I was on a rock just above Horse Point with the expanse of Wingletang Down behind me. The Western Rocks lay about three miles in front of me and the Bishop Rock Lighthouse a further two. I was thinking of all the lives that had been lost to those rocks: people from all over the world, taken by surprise and flung into the gullet of the sea. I must have gone into a daydream. When I came round, I could see tens of yachts flirting with the Western Rocks. Sails of all colours were pushing through the sea. I imagined all the ghosts of the drowned kneeling on the rocks, waving shirts and rags, warning off the yachtsmen, screaming into the wind and the flying surf as the sails came nearer and nearer. Later, I heard that it was the Fastnet race I had been witnessing.

A posse of fidgety gulls were psyching themselves up for a raid on the remains of my lunch. They were busily being inconspicuous like a man waiting to pick up a five pound note from the pavement. The cricketers had stopped for tea which made the gulls even more anxious to have theirs: so I got up and left them to it.

After one more pint at the Turk's Head I was ready to board the boat at Porth Conger, little realising that I would be on the same spot again sooner than I thought. The skipper and his mate unloaded the island supplies onto the thin finger of the quay and islanders and visitors promptly filled up the seats. I noticed, not without irony, a big box of chocolate flavoured soya dessert sitting on the quay and to this day I still have not sampled a Turk's Head pasty.

The fine day was turning into an equally fine evening. It was a Wednesday and as on all Wednesday evenings in the Summer, it was the women's gig race night. For a small charge, you can follow the rowers in one of the pleasure boats. That night, they were racing from St Mary's to St Agnes. Following the race is a very popular after-dinner pastime or, if you eat late, a stimulant for a big appetite. Hundreds of people converge on the quay, queuing up to board their chosen launch. When everybody is settled in, the boats chug out to the starting line, meeting up with other off-island spectators. The gigs are manoeuvred back and forth until they are all lined up. The best races can have about seven or eight gigs racing and plenty of shady bets and light flutters are contracted in the few minutes before the start. Most people call the gigs by their colours, which seems a shame when they have names like Nournor, Bonnet, Golden Eagle and Serica. The spectators cheer on their favourite gigs as their grandstands plough through the sea. Arms are waved and encouragement shouted with all the excitement of Newmarket. Everybody cheers as the winning gig crosses the line.

Applause is given for the losing teams with an extra boost for the last. The oars are raised in the winning gig to the delight of the spectators. Most of the launches return to their respective islands except for the one which calls into Porth Conger on St Agnes.

That night in the Turk's Head after a few beers, an announcement was made that the St Mary's launch was about to return. Drinks were downed and our St Mary's contingent made for the quay where a tow rope had been attached from the launch to the gig. It was dark by then and we clambered aboard the launch in high spirits. Off we chugged across the Sound, singing songs into the darkness with the St Mary's gig dragging along behind, full of jubilant rowers.

Chapter Four

People have boats on the Isles of Scilly the way Londoners have cars. During the winter, tiny craft are pulled up above the beaches or put under wraps in backyards. Adverts go up in shop windows for boats of all kinds with the promise of excitement and adventure: the excitement of pushing off from the flat sands of Porth Mellon, drifting across St Mary's Pool until the winds fill out the sails of a small yacht...the adventure of landing on a deserted beach with provisions for the day, then later, quietly stealing back into Hugh Town harbour under the cover of darkness. And only three hundred and fifty miles away, thousands of people squash together, incarcerated inside the London underground system, avoiding the gaze of their fellow travellers and reading advertisements for phone-in horoscopes.

Access to a boat opens up a whole new dimension. Islands which before were just gazed upon from a pleasure boat trip become tantalising possibilities. These little islands are addictive. Once a grain of sand gets under your toenail and into your bloodstream, the likelihood is that you will develop full blown islomania. I doubt if there is any drug that can give me a buzz or blow my mind to the same degree as standing on the top of a twenty acre island. With the sea stretched out below me and the sky stretched out above me, my thoughts, cheese sandwiches and the whirling sea birds for company, I can sit on an island totally alone. Alone yet not lonely.

The two main groups of deserted islands to explore are the Eastern Isles and the cluster which lie between St Martin's and Tresco. Tean, St Helen's, Northwethel and Round Island are the major islands of the latter group, the rest being either rocks, ledges or sandbars. With its sprawling fingers, Tean has the appearance of a spillage of ink in some clumsy boy's schoolbook. Most of the beaches are stripped away at high tide leaving just the bare bones of Tean stranded and cold. The fern and bracken reach over six foot in some places making a cross-country trip extremely tiring, especially on a hot day. I visited Tean with some archaeologist friends once, who, after landing on the north-west side, strolled out across the exposed sands of West Porth to look for a submerged cairn. To their great delight the tide was far enough out to enable them to have a good butchers at it. How strange it is that a burial tomb built thousands of years ago to house the remains of some important person should in this day and age be playing peek-a-boo with a party of archaeologists. What must Scilly have been like when, less than three thousand years ago, all the islands apart from the Western Rocks, Annet and St Agnes were one large island? Wouldn't it be amazing if Scilly could get hold of that little Oriental boy who can swallow up whole oceans in one slurp? I am sure the waters of Scilly wouldn't detain him for long.

Two of my companions, Jim and Jill Crump, were determined to seek out Crump Island on the southern tip of Tean. The tide was still a fair way out so we made our way across the sands of East Porth towards the sandbar which connected Crump Island to Tean. It was more of an overgrown rock than an island but to the visiting Crumps, it was a sacred place of pilgrimage. The three of us stood on the hot sandbar looking at the island which was now high and dry. "So. Crump Island." said Jill. "Yes," said Jim, "Crump Island." The two of them stood there with their own thoughts. I gestured towards the rock like some mercenary guide delivering the goods. "Well, I suppose you had better climb it."

"Right then," said Jim. "Let's go."

Reaching the compact summit of Crump Island did not take more than a few minutes. Most of it is submerged at high tide leaving a mass of rock thirty feet high with a plateau of springy turf just big enough to accommodate a two -person tent. Jim and Jill stood on top of the highest boulder and looked out across the waters with an almost territorial devotion. In true Everest tradition, I took a photograph of the pair of them standing proudly on their summit. "This will make the front page of the Guardian," I joked. "Yes, 'Crump on Crump Island'". I left them with their own thoughts and rejoined the others with their cairn.

Chapter Five

The ten acre island of Northwethel lies just west of Tean and induced the response, "You're not going there! A whole day, but there's nothing out there!" Suddenly, I felt uneasy. A whole day on ten acres. I knew I was right and that he was wrong but I bought an extra portion of garlic sausage just in case. Just in case of what I was not sure but it made me feel better and I walked off excitedly to meet my fellow travellers on the quay. Cathy Parks, an archaeologist, was waiting with her red and white javelin, along with another friend, Mark Porter, head waiter at the Star Castle Hotel. Alec Hicks gave us a wave from his boat 'Gloria' and we made our way down the old granite steps of the quay. Also on the boat was a party of people Alec was taking fishing east of the Eastern Isles. One of them, a middle-aged man in a Barbour jacket, gestured to Cathy's ranging pole. "You won't catch many fish with that, my dear." Cathy smiled politely. "She spears them," said Mark. "Deadly, she is." The wind off the sea was welcome that day, along with the spray of surf tingling our faces.

We climbed up the Sound past Tobaccoman's Point and slowly past Tea Ledge, Great Cheese Rock and Little Cheese Rock. Tean was on our right and Crump Island was little more than a knuckle of rock. Alec rowed the three of us in his dinghy from the 'Gloria' to the southern end of Northwethel. The landing beach was a mass of seaweed-smothered rocks and, with the aid of Cathy's very versatile ranging pole, we slipped and slid across to the civility of the sandy beach. Cathy bade us farewell and wandered off with her ranging pole and maps to discover a few ancient monuments. We said that there might be a fair chance of us bumping into each other during the course of the day but if not, we would see her there again at five. Cathy had all the maps so Mark and I had to do without.

Most of Northwethel, like the other uninhabited islands, is covered in a healthy growth of bracken and fern. Like Samson and Great Ganilly, Northwethel consists of two hills connected by a low stretch of land. We could have walked round it in half an hour but doing so would have meant missing its caves, its pot holes, curiously shaped rocks and fragile worlds in its many rock pools. We made our way along the west coast. We could see the pines of Tresco stretched along Castle Down and the Island Hotel at Old Grimsby just a quarter of a mile away. A small red fishing boat chugged its way up through the dividing channel. The fisherman was at the back of the boat attending to some fish crates.

When on a seldom visited island, my natural interest in beachcombing intensifies. What could have washed up since the last time somebody was here is anybody's guess. Only once have I ever found a message in a bottle. That was at the Birling Gap in Sussex. I was six years old and picked up a bottle containing crude drawings by someone not much older than myself. I passed the crayoned genitals to my mother, much to her disgust, who threw them back into the sea.

There were the usual bundles of fishing nets and rounded bits of polystyrene. The ubiquitous mineral water bottles and sticky pools of jelled gunge were abundant as were the Spanish sherry bottles and bits of crate. Further up the coast was a large piece of rusting ship, rough and contorted after being spat out by the sea. The beach disappeared into a series of mousehole caves just before the northern hill began to rise and progress was made by clambering up onto the grassy bank above the caves. Time was passing by nicely. Millions had been made and lost on London's stock market but we were content with our picnic of bread, cheese, beer and garlic sausage. The tide was completely out. Rocks and sandbars blinked in the dazzling afternoon sun. Jaded shellfish closed their lids and bands of shining seaweed reached for the elusive waves.

After my picnic, with pride and exhilaration I reached the top of Northwethel, a sheer-sided cube of granite. I soon forgot about my prowess when faced with the view of St Helen's. Tresco, St Martin's and Tean could be seen but the hump of St Helen's stole the show. What a huge green rounded thing it is, soft and feminine, the way it would fill your palms. It looked like a good place. Not good for anything in particular, just a good place.

From its west coast, a narrow carpet of grey, glistening boulders had been rolled out half a mile long: the Golden Ball Brow. Another half a mile of carpet remained to be laid but that would have to wait: the tide was turning. Beyond the Golden Ball Brow stood Men-a-vaur with its towering blades of parallel rock shooting straight out of the sea for over a hundred feet.

Like the man who climbed a cliff to fill his basket full of eggs I sat on top of Northwethel wondering how the hell I would get down. Even more intrigued, I wondered how the hell I had got up. Pretending that there were eggs at the bottom of the rock seemed the only way. Halfway down and glued to the granite with the sweat from my fingers, I wondered if this would be the place where I would meet my end. I had seen many worse places in which to end one's life and I suddenly thought of what my old headmistress' reaction would be if she were to hear that I had fallen to my death on Northwethel. It's strange, the thoughts that flit across one's mind in these small places of the sea. Clocks have no currency in these places and they treat the intrusion of humans with the nonchalance of a cabinet minister.

On the southern hill of Northwethel we could see the primitive shape of Cathy stalking around with her spear, inspecting a cairn like a woman of those old times revisiting her lost past. The tide was gaining ground, swallowing up insular worlds as it went. Display case rock pools shuddered, leaving us with sea-stained feet before a mad dash to dry land. Huge plump boulders gave us kip. Cathy joined us after her work and the three of us lay pinned to the smooth rock under the pressure of sunshine.

Lazily, we strolled back to the landing place. There was no sign of the 'Gloria'. Mark stretched himself out on top of a boulder continuing where he had left off. Cathy sat on the sand scratching runic designs into a large rock and I sat at the water's edge throwing stones into the sea. Somebody had to throw stones into the sea so I thought it might as well be me. The small red fishing boat was now chugging down the channel. The fisherman was in the back of the boat, working his knife through the silvery bellies of mackerel. Alec followed soon and this time we started with Little Cheese Rock and finished with Tobacco Man's Point; a much more agreeable arrangement.

Chapter Six

A low mist sponged the islands. The 'Gloria' nosed out gently from Hugh Town harbour. Once again we were heading for those secret islands between St Martin's and Tresco, this time to St Helen's. There was only one other person on the boat apart from Alec Hicks and that was Cathy.

It was a ghostly trip, rocks appeared and disappeared. The only sounds were that of the boat's engine and the muted remarks of bemused seabirds. Nobody spoke. The mist lifted slightly and we could see the Abbey on Tresco surrounded by its pines. It was as if the roof of the sky had dropped, reducing the dimension of up, to mere feet and inches.

Light rain had joined the mist by the time we reached St Helen's. Visibility was a couple of hundred feet. As we watched Alec disappear in his boat, I suddenly thought "What the hell am I doing here?" Cathy disappeared in her usual manner with her maps and ranging pole and I stood on the beach with my cameras, a plastic carrier bag of food and a vague lunch appointment for about one o'clock.

We had landed on the southern end of the island on a sandbar which disappears every twelve hours or so. In front of me was Tean and Northwethel with St Mary's hiding away somewhere in the distance. Behind me, the steep butt of St Helen's rose to its rounded top, hiding from view its more genteel proportions. A few yards up from the beach amongst the bracken and brambles nestled a derelict granite building - a square room with a lean-to built on one side. The roof was long gone and its red brick chimney sat tall and naked. Its walls were complete, its large windows just empty sockets, a roofless skull staring mindlessly out across St Helen's pool. I knew well what it was, its grim past and wretched inhabitants. They call it 'the Pest House'. In the days of the plague, infected sailors were locked up inside the small room which served as a quarantine station.

I walked in through the empty doorway and stood in the middle of the room. The ground was not as overgrown as I had imagined. I thought about those stricken sailors who must have been thankful for the large, staring windows. An estate agent might refer to them as picture windows during his sales pitch and comment on the compact nature of the residence. Patches of plaster still clung to the walls. A few white feathers twitched in the bottom of the fireplace. I became uneasy. All that disease - the Plague, Black Death - in these small confines. Could the bugs still be around, hiding in the cracks the way I had once imagined them to be alive in the mass graves underneath the football pitches on Blackheath? I knew it was not possible, the germs were dead. But something lingered on.

The drizzle had stopped, the mist was rising, the sun was waiting. I left the Pest House and followed a path through the bracken towards the steep rise. I was looking for a saint's hut: St Elid's hut. It may only be a hut to us but to St Elid it was home. A few feet away was a ruined monastery built in his name. It must be nice to have a monastery named after you. I sat on its flowering, humble altar. The walls were barely three feet high, mossy and damp. I felt pretty conspicuous sitting on the altar with my Co-op bag and cameras. There was nobody there to see me, the gulls didn't seem to take any notice but I felt uncomfortable so I invited myself round to St Elid's place for a spot of light lunch. The hut left a lot to be desired. For a start, there was no roof. The circular wall reached only knee height and there was no front door. I knew that St Elid was buried in the ground not so far away so I admired what was left of the hut and wondered if one built in the twentieth century would be in such good nick after fourteen hundred years or so.

The bracken was thick all the way up the south side of the island's rise. Once at the top, a thick bouncy growth of grass took over. In the distance, I could see Cathy with her ranging pole, standing upright like a one-armed Man of Wilmington. Beyond her was the pale green expanse of sea, clear to the northern horizon. I turned round but St Mary's was still just a faint stain in the mingling sea and sky.

The Golden Ball Brow was submerged. Men-a-vaur stood holding its breath like a bather in cold water. To the north, I could see the white tower of Round Island Lighthouse just rising above the outline of St Helen's. At night, the red eye of the lighthouse used to sweep its beam across the islands. It was still operated by people at that time. Since then, computers have been installed and silicon chips send out a beam of white, unseeing light. From the north-east coast of St Helen's, Round Island could be seen scuttling off like a beaver, as if on a long journey to the Irish coast.

I met up with Cathy and we had lunch on the northern slopes, looking across to Men-a-vaur. We had the island to ourselves: all fifty acres of it. A long red oil tanker lay in the distant sea. It had disappeared behind Men-a-vaur and then reappeared by the time we had finished eating, moving anxiously along like the last duck in a shooting gallery. The Pest House and saint's hut were out of sight, at the back of the island, at the back of the mind. That end of St Helen's was still under mist. The winds blew fresh on our northern end. We could see the horizon. All was clear.

I remained on the top half of the island for the rest of the afternoon exploring the slippery grass slopes and the boulderous coast, pleasing myself with this and that so that Cathy had to call me as to a little boy when it was time for Alec to pick us up. We reached the Pest House. Visibility had greatly improved since the morning. The chimney of St Mary's power station could be picked out as could the B.B.C. radio mast three miles away. There was no sign of Alec. We sat on rocks set in the grass. Alongside were blackberry bushes and behind those, the Pest House.

"I wonder if those poor buggers in the Pest House used to eat blackberries?" I thought it was a reasonable question but Cathy didn't seem over-impressed. "I don't know about them, but if Alec doesn't turn up then I know two people who definitely will be eating blackberries." There was an air of seriousness in Cathy's delivery."Alec wouldn't leave us, would he?" I pleaded. "He wouldn't leave us stranded, with no food or shelter. Things like that only happen in books." Half of me quite liked the idea of being stranded on a deserted island while the other half very much liked the idea of quietly supping beer in the warmth of the Mermaid. "Well, it's not impossible. We wouldn't be the first." A million and one things went through my head in the next thirty seconds as I scanned the waters for the 'Gloria'. As if to give her worries some credibility, Cathy went on to tell the story of a college student who was stranded on Samson for two days.

"It happened a few years ago. He was out there doing some drawings of the cairns. Come five o'clock, he went down to the landing beach and waited for the boat to pick him up. Of course, it never turned up. He decided to build a shelter inside one of the ruined cottages. The next morning he went to the top of South Hill with his ranging pole, tied the arms of a shirt to the end of it and waited for the morning's traffic. But whenever a boat came into view and he waved his flag at them, they all just waved back at him thinking he was having a joke. That's how it went for the rest of the day until he retreated back to the shelter. It was only because he lit a fire the next day that a boat decided to find out what was going on."

We both looked out across St Helen's Pool. There was no sign of Alec, his boat or anybody else's. It was six-thirty. By seven, we had finished off my packet of KP honey roasted peanuts and the explanation for the large sheet of yellow tarpaulin tied up in the lean-to of the Pest House was slowly dawning. The Pest House stood like a worldly wise butler, silent and inevitable. It was starting to turn cold. Soon we would have to talk of other things, practical and down-to-earth things. Soon, the lights of Hugh Town would be winking at us. "Can you hear a noise?" No, I could not. "It sounds like an engine."

"You are beginning to be effected. I can't hear anything."

"Look, look!" she shouted, "It's a boat !" She was right. It was the 'Gloria'. Half of me was excited with relief whilst the rest of me was quietly disappointed. It appeared that Alec had decided to take some people fishing out past the Eastern Isles. We were glad to see him. He looked at us, slightly amused, as we clambered aboard the 'Gloria'. "Thought I'd forgotten all about you, eh?"

"The thought did cross our minds," replied Cathy. Alec grinned all the way back to Hugh Town.

We went back via Tresco Channel past Piper's Hole, Kettle Point and Gimble Point in between Tresco and Bryher. We approached Hangman Island. Silhouetted against the fading light of the sky were the gallows, thin and deadly. Admiral Blake is said to have snapped many a neck on that towering rock. But these gallows were only a few weeks old; 'Hollywood' gallows, constructed by the film crew who were making an adaptation of the book, 'Why the Whales Came'. It was very convincing, as if the ghost of the gallows had come back to haunt, even if its victims were content to rest. I'm sure Alec had his reasons for taking that particular route back, but for me, it just made the warmth of the Mermaid even more desirable.

Chapter Seven

St Martin's is often looked upon as the least interesting of the inhabited islands. Some people have gone so far as to say, "Oh, I'm not going to St Martin's - it's boring." It is true that some islands flaunt their attractions with gay abandon while others, like St Martin's, take a more philosophical attitude. If you want to explore St Martin's, then do. If you don't fancy it, then that's no problem. You pays your money and you takes your choice. I wouldn't recommend St Martin's to somebody who wants to run away from problems or forget about things. The problems will very likely follow and dog them for their entire stay. On the other hand, if you want to 'get your head together' then the island is the perfect place. The more I visit St Martin's, the more I love it.

Geologically, St Martin's has no similarities to the South Downs in Sussex but I am always reminded of them when walking along the island's ridged backbone. I used to love starting out from Eastbourne, walking along the ridge to Jevington, stopping for a pint and then on to Alfriston and the Long Man of Wilmington. It felt good standing on the hill overlooking Eastbourne. It felt good to know that the ridge of hills I was standing on reached all the way to Arundel and somehow I felt connected to both towns - the way I feel connected to both ends of St Martin's when standing on either end of its banana-shaped ridge.

I got incredibly sunburnt on St Martin's. The sky was open, ultra-violet rays hit the ground like stair rods and the heather buzzed with all the heat. I had walked along the entire coast of the island and had returned to Great Bay on the northern side with picnic provisions bought from the Post Office-cum-General Stores in Higher Town. I sat on the perfect sands which made up the half mile sweep of Great and Little Bay. The ridge rose up from the beach like a private grandstand. There were not many spectators and only a French yacht party and I crowded the sands. The water was so clear. I could see the sea bed for a long way off-shore. Reefs of dark green seaweed were mooching about in the polarised water. The French yacht, gleaming and white, seemed suspended in mid-air. I lay there in the shade, tentatively applying suntan lotion to my burnt bits. There was no aftersun lotion in the Post Office, only suntan lotion. I didn't think that the grade two lotion would provide much relief. I probably needed something like grade nine. I longed to put something cold and soothing over my burns and wished that the Post Office sold those Tetra Brik packets of soya dessert. Even on overcast days, the sun's burning rays penetrate and some people have to resort to the protection of cardboard armoury perched on their burnt noses. It was all too hot and I was gasping for a cup of tea so I made tracks to the Polreath Tea Room.

The Polreath Tea Room is situated at Higher Town. People sit at picnic benches in the open sunshine or huddle together in the Tea Room in damp clusters, with steam rising from their coats and cups of strong tea. Elderly ladies sit at the sun-warmed picnic tables eating homemade chocolate gateau and shooing small birds away.

That day, me and my sunburn had decided to go for the chocolate gateau. Geoff Watts, who with his wife and children run the Tea Room, cut me a large wedge out of the cake. I sat outside on the grass and watched the old ladies flicking their wrists at the birds and making sure the crumbs fell onto the plate. I leant back against a wall, sipping tea and eating cake. Opposite me on the grass was a party of five people quietly chatting away amongst themselves. Binoculars hung from their necks and a telescope lay on the grass next to their large pot of tea. "Spotted anything interesting?" I asked. A thin tall man wearing a Stetson replied "No, nothing much, just the usual. It's been a bloody fine day though." He was right. Not a puff of wind. The kind of day you could count on your fingers.

Refreshed after the tea and cake, I left the bird watchers and the old ladies and headed off towards the eastern end of the island where the large red and white stripped Daymark stands. A few steps along the lane and I was standing in front of a collection of small signs attached to a stone wall (or hedge as they are called in Scilly). This, then, is the Tourist Information Centre.

Further along the 'main' road, I met a British Telecom man proudly painting one of the island's two telephone boxes. It was the perfect day for painting telephone boxes and I dare say the man from B.T. was enjoying himself immensely, taking great care not to get paint on the tiny windows. I asked him what I would have to do if I wanted to make a call. "If you wanted to make a call..." repeated the man. "Well, I dare say, if you were very careful, didn't spoil my paint job and didn't mind me overhearing you, then you could use this box. On the other hand, you could walk down to Middle Town and use the box there. Otherwise, you'd just have to wait for the paint to dry." Luckily, I didn't want to make a call. I wished him well with his painting and continued along the lane.

The lane was getting narrower, slowly winding upwards past allotments of cabbages and brocolli. On my left, I stopped to admire a shed. Its wooden door faced onto the lane. It was bolted, and painted on its surface were the words 'RETIRED FROM ACTIVE SERVICE, 8.30 p.m., 26.8.85. R.I.P'. This, I later found out, was the shed which housed the island's electricity generator, now defunct due to the mains cable being laid from St Mary's.

The lane which was now a dirt path climbed out into an expanse of thick grass and stone walls. St Mary's lay a couple of miles across Crow Sound to the south. In front of me, seemingly at touching distance, lay the green clutch of the Eastern Isles. I was now walking along the open ridge of St Martin's towards Chapel Down. Not surprisingly, there used to be a chapel on Chapel Down. There still is, or what remains of it. Ruined cottages sit dissolving into the heather and gorse. Alongside are the remains of a field system long neglected, ravaged by wind and sun. This headland drops one hundred and sixty feet into the sea. It's an open place, left to the whims of the weather and the wondering thoughts of Man.

I had reached the Daymark, often described as rocket shaped. It's a good description and will be so until one day it surprises us all and blasts off into outer space. It looks modern but in fact was erected in 1683. On the side of the Daymark the date 1637 has been marked and I wondered whether this was due to the slow pace of life of St Martin's, forty six years behind everybody else. I stood on the concrete plateau right on the edge of the headland, as most people tend to do when in the area. I could see the clear horizontal pencil of the mainland, twenty eight miles away across the Atlantic Ocean: Land's End, Sennen and Cape Cornwall. I could see the white specks of buildings. I tried to imagine the entire U.K. mainland wrapped around the globe, out of sight like somebody trying to climb the other side of a wall.

I walked across the ancient fields to the southern end of Chapel Down. The nearest of the Eastern Isles, Nornour, lay less than half a mile away. I sat myself on top of an exposed burial chamber and applied some more of the grade two suntan lotion. Lying almost at my feet was an ancient stone idol carved thousands of years ago by an unknown hand. Its exact location had left human memory about forty years ago. All that was known was the fact that it existed, somewhere out there on wild Chapel Down. It was pointed out to me by an archaeologist shortly after it was rediscovered in 1988. It was considerably worn, but there it was, without a doubt, the long lost stone idol, wondering what all the fuss was about and getting bored of having its photograph taken.

I, like everybody else, was ignorant of the idol's whereabouts and probably stepped on its nose as I rose from the chamber and continued on my way. I headed back to Higher Town and the Polreath Tea Room. I was staying at the Polreath Guest House, Geoff Watts had said dinner was at seven thirty and I had just enough time to get back and have a shower.

I woke up the next morning with my head full of talk from the previous evening's conversation: stories of ghosts wandering the shores searching for lost relatives and rats running wild in the dead of night. In fact, I was sure someone had said rat infested. "White Island is rat infested." That's what they had said. I didn't mention that I intended to go to White Island or that I was even thinking about staying the night out there. I just listened, thinking twice about my plans. It wasn't so much the talk of ghosts. I had never seen a ghost so wasn't worried. It was the talk of rats which bugged me. I had seen rats and I didn't like them. The thought of spending a night on a rat- infested island did not appeal. I wanted to go to White Island because at low tide it is possible to walk across the rocky causeway which links it to St Martin's. This is what did appeal. I suppose it was something to do with the 'something for nothing' philosophy.

I set off, with my breakfast inside me and a liberal coating of newly acquired lotion spread on my burnt bits, out into another scorcher of a day. There was a slight breeze tickling the palms of Higher Town. The telephone box was dry and the contingent of small birds were gathering in anticipation of the first boatload of visitors. I took the path down alongside Great and Little Bays, stopping to look at the white yacht which was giving out a curious cowbell sound as it swayed gently from side to side. White Island lay off the northern point of St Martin's and already, much of the causeway was exposed. Low tide was just after eleven. There was no rush as the island was accessible for some time before and after. It did not look like a rat-infested island but then, appearances do sometimes deceive - take Puffin Island, for instance, off the coast of Anglesey in Wales, where the massive rat population is literally eating its way down the west side of the island to the south side.

I decided to have a mid-morning snack before crossing over to White Island. After doing a quick stock-take of my provisions I issued myself with a small carton of orange juice and tin of Skipjack tuna fish (in brine). I sat down on the small headland where the causeway joins St Martin's, fringed with marram grass and littered with names. 'Tom', 'Carol', 'Julie', and many others, all spelt out with large stones set into the springy turf. How old the names were I hadn't a clue. Maybe if they survive long enough, today's "thoughtless defacing of the landscape" will be tomorrow's ancient monument. As well as names there were a few spirals, some of them quite large, enjoying that settled feeling that comes with age. For some reason, all those names and spirals had congregated there, on that small grassy headland.

The last time I visited the headland, 'Tom' was looking the worse for wear. 'Carol' and 'Julie' had disappeared. In their place were 'Peter', 'Sam', 'Nanny' and 'Boysie'. The spirals remained untouched. They looked set to see out the century. The names come and go the way you would think it was the winter waves that had swept up the stones, rearranging them into new names.

Picking my way across the slippery, seaweed-smothered boulders, I was still undecided as to whether or not I was going to sleep rough that night. After climbing up a large lump of granite, I scrambled up a grassy bank onto the footpath. A group of snooty seagulls crawed indignantly before flying off towards Round Island. My eyes followed them for a time. If it wasn't for me they would still have been there sitting in the grass, gossiping. To the left of Round Island was St Helen's, with the tall shape of Men-a-vaur in between. Northwethel and Tean were both hidden from view by Top Rock Hill at the other end of the causeway above the names and spirals.

White Island is about half a mile long and shaped like a pistol grip. The back of the handle is flanked by a stretch of sand and boulders. The sand was hot and the dry granules made it hard going. Back on the footpath I came across something of which I had heard people talk: a kelp pit - a shallow round pit about four feet across lined with small boulders. They were last used in the nineteenth century. Twenty tons of seaweed had to be burnt to produce one ton of kelp, which would fetch from three to five pounds. Just imagine, some forty or fifty pits smoking away in unison. The stench must have been horrendous.

I reached the flat grassy expanse which separated the two hills, one on the northern end, the other on the southern end of the island. This would be the place to build a house if you intended to make the island your home. There is an ancient field system here but to me it remained illusive. The flat expanse was about the size of a football pitch, joining the east to the west coast. Up above in front of me sat a high green ridge with a few outcrops of granite poking into the horizon. I slowly drew my gaze along its sharp outline. "Injun country," I said aloud. I withdrew my line of sight slowly down the hillside towards me. It was high noon. The shadows had retreated underneath the rocks. The tide was advancing. My gaze dropped into the grass surrounding me. "Rats," I said aloud. I looked around for evidence of their occupancy. There were lengths of orange nylon rope, shampoo bottles and bits of rounded polystyrene. There were no rat droppings. Millions of rabbit droppings but no rat droppings. I was safe.

I walked up to the top of the ridge where I found a nicely sprung sea pink. I sat on the sea pink and watched. The tide was gradually gnawing its way through the connection, each wave doing its duty in a time-honoured ceremony. I could see Tean, Northwethel, St Helen's, Men-a-vaur and Round Island. To the north, there were 180 degrees of nothing...Well, if you can call 180 degrees of Atlantic Ocean and a few miles of headroom with a couple of clouds as walk-on extras nothing, then there was nothing. I moved down the slope a little way so I could stretch myself out fully and still watch the causeway dissolving. Also lying on the gentle gradient a few feet away was an empty plastic bottle of Iron Brew. The air inside the bottle was hot, condensation trickled down the insides. I sucked my tongue and reached for a carton of orange juice. I lay back and drank. The sun was bold and naked. Seagulls flew out of it like attacking Messerschmitts. My arms and legs were protected from the sun but from the seagulls I had no defence. I sustained a direct hit to my left leg and cursed out loud in response. The gull flew off towards Round Island.

I could feel time slipping away like sand in an hour glass. Soon the two seas would meet. White Island would indeed be an island once again. It felt good.

It was nearly four o'clock. The umbilical cord had broken. I was alone. I was the prisoner, held captive by natural forces. I knew rightly that if all was well with the world tomorrow, the sea would part and I would walk free.

As far as I was concerned I was the king of the castle. White Island belonged to Me and nobody could dispute it. I could even change its name. Blue Island, Red Island, Green with Brown and Purple Spots Island, the possibilities were limitless. I pondered on these thoughts, slowly emptying the litre of orange juice. With all that freedom I was contented to just lie there in the sun, knowing that if I wanted to I could do just what I fancied. Bliss.

The delicate veil of evening was slowly drawing in. Finding a suitable place to sleep seemed a good idea. I stood up and studied the island from my high vantage point. South of the ridge, the land sloped down towards the flat middle section of the island, then rose again to form the southern hill. The northern slope of the ridge banked out to form something like half an amphitheatre. The northern bowl looked inviting, secluded. The turf must have been sprung by a mattress manufacturer. I rolled out my sleeping bag, undressed and slid into the warm envelope of eiderdown. It was still early but as there seemed to be a total lack of local night life, I decided to call it an early night. Before I turned in I munched an apple and threw the core to one side, leaving it as an experiment for the 'rat-infested' theory. The silver light from the three quarter moon touched the island and the surrounding sea. There I was, alone; but not for long.

I woke up to the sound of something being dragged along. The moon had moved, it must have been about eleven o'clock. I sat up with my ears pricked. It sounded as if it was something heavy. The sound would stop for a few seconds, then start again. I dressed and climbed to the top of the ridge. The noise grew louder. I stood behind a granite outcrop and waited for my eyes to become accustomed to the light. The noise stopped. I waited a few minutes and was just thinking about going back to bed when it started again. It was coming from the western beach. I could see a figure, a grey figure, dragging along behind something large and long. My eyes were straining to pick out the details. The figure was having difficulty pulling its load up from the beach and onto the flat grass. Once manoeuvred, it continued to drag the load right across to the east side of the island. The grey figure walked back alone and stood on the beach looking west. I remained at my look-out post wondering what the bloody hell was going on. I went for a pee behind the outcrop. When I had finished, the figure had gone. I looked up and down the beach but there was no sign. I waited for a long time. It was probably only ten minutes but it seemed like a long time. Nothing stirred. I went back to bed. I slept deeply and rose early.

There were no shadows in the morning, the sun was weak. A relief for my sunburn. The sea was open and wide; so calm. The seagulls could not be bothered with flying so they just sat around on rocks looking stupid. I dressed, rolled up my sleeping bag and gathered up my things. The apple core was still lying where I had thrown it. I walked over. It was untouched - not even the slightest nibble.

I spent the morning exploring the east coast. Great semi-circles of land had been bitten away by the sea. Watery caves hid away inside the hard granite. Some were inaccessible without a boat, others were high and dry. Inside one cave grew a display of mosses and ferns, green and humid. Others were dry and dead. Eventually I arrived at the place where the grey figure had left its load on the east coast at Stony Porth. I sat on the grassy edge with the sea some fifteen feet below me. It had been high tide and low tide and high tide again since my crossing the day before. There was no sign of the grey figure's activity. I looked at the sea and let it lie there, leaving the episode of the grey figure as one of those strange goings-on that are part and parcel of small islands.

The causeway was busily getting itself together in time for low tide. The first few boulders were poking their heads into the mid-morning air. On St Martin's, I could see a black figure sitting on a large boulder. For somewhere so quiet and out of the way there seemed to be a lot of goings on. As the tide receded the black figure stirred itself and began to pick its route across the wet causeway. The black shape looked to me like a clergyman, his long robe hung about him in the still air. I opened a bottle of beer, drank slowly and watched with some curiosity the advancing man of the cloth. I had never been visited by one of his type before. I looked at my remaining food stock to see what I could offer him. He disappeared out of view for a while as he climbed onto White Island and made his way along the footpath. He reappeared and as he got nearer I realised that he was heading towards me.

"Good morning," I said, after taking a drag from the bottle. He returned the greeting and stopped a few feet away from me."Were you stranded?" he asked. "No, I did it on purpose."

"Oh, that's all right then, as long as you know what you're doing." We sat together on the grassy edge eating bread and cheese, discussing the ways of the world. "I'm a relief priest," he said, waving a hunk of bread in front of his face. "I'm over here for a couple of weeks."

"Where are you normally?"

"Streatham in London." The idea of a relief priest from Streatham appealed. I offered him a swig of beer. He declined. There sat the two of us, the relief priest from Streatham and me.

Both sea and sky were grey. A moderate breeze blew into our faces, the bread and cheese were eaten. I gathered my things and stood up. "Well, see you Guv'."

"Yes, good-bye. Might see you again some time."

"Don't get caught by the tide, will you?"

"Only if I want to John." With that, I strolled off towards the causeway, crossed and continued onwards along the path to Higher Town.

The white French yacht had sailed away, the path was empty. Soon I had rejoined the island's one and only road and strolled off down to the quay to catch the boat back to St Mary's.

Chapter Eight

We waited three weeks for the right sea, weather and tidal conditions to take a trip out to Rosevear and land. There were six of us all together: Alec the boatman, Cathy and her ranging pole, three other archaeologists and me. Rosevear, the largest of the Western Rocks, five miles west of Hugh Town quay; the refinement of solitude. In 1847 a small colony of workmen invaded and erected sheds for workshops and granite huts for living quarters, then set about spending the next seven years building the Bishop Rock Lighthouse a further two miles out in the Atlantic.

One fine August evening the word was spread. "It's on." Within half an hour we were all gathered on the quay in anticipation. Alec helped us into the 'Gloria' then off we chugged into the evening, complete with cameras, maps, diagrams, notepads, ranging poles and flasks of coffee. "You know you can only land for half an hour?" said Alec. We all nodded. "If you get stuck out there you'll have to wait for high tide again and maybe the sea will be too rough to pick you up." Once again we all nodded. The light was soft and golden, the sea shiny with the sky's powder blue reflection. Noisily, we cut through the open sea. The 'Gloria' was going full pelt and everything shook - if it didn't shake it rattled, including our teeth. St Agnes and Gugh were having a rest from each other's company. The white thumb of St Agnes Lighthouse was giving us the okay. Onward we ploughed towards Annet. We could see the familiar sight of the Haycocks reaching out from the northern tip of Annet, a line of massive triangular rocks from which they take their name. From their rocky, white splattered vantage points the anxious shapes of shags and cormorants were keeping a beady eye on us. Seals bobbed their heads through the slow waters checking on our progress, and silent gulls followed our stern.

Past the Haycocks, clear of the Ranneys and we were in the pallet of the Western Rocks. The two mile wide jaw of teeth grinned at us. In the order of teeth, Rosevear would rank as right canine, Melledgan and Gorregan would be the front teeth and the back teeth would consist of Hellweathers, Menrounds and The Brow opposed by Great and Little Crebawethan, Jacky's Rock and Silver Carn.

Maps were studied and notebooks primed as we approached the dividing channel between Rosevean and Rosevear. We could see the ruined gables of one of the granite huts just rising above the island's boulderous coastline. The 'Gloria' slowed to a gentle halt in the relatively calm sea. Alec untied the dinghy from the boat's stern, brought it round to the starboard side and one by one we climbed in. Once settled, we checked all of our bits and pieces and those of us who had watches synchronised them. The archaeologists had half an hour to carry out their raid: everything was planned. I had no plan and no watch, just an open mind and a happy-go-lucky attitude. Alec rowed us to the boulderous shore and steadied the dinghy next to a small shelf of granite a couple of feet above the slopping waves. "Right, here we are. You are going to have to jump." I detected a slight tinge of amusement in his delivery. I was sitting nearest the ledge and so was the first to jump. Alec paddled around with his oars controlling the dinghy. I stood on the port side waiting to pick my moment. The dinghy rocked as I safely landed on the wet ledge. For one moment I was on Rosevear and the rest of them were still afloat. We looked at each other.

Cathy was next, followed by the others. Alec remained in the dinghy and rowed back to the 'Gloria' after giving us one last warning about the tides. I was already making tracks.

There was no wind. The sun was starting to dive into the sea. In an hour it would be gone. Rosevear was peaceful, a deserted battlefield. Amongst the rocks and cracked earth lay the decaying carcasses of dead sea birds. Up in front of me in a small forest of tree mallow sat the walled remains of a stone workshop. This, then, was the place where the men who built Britain's tallest lighthouse lived and worked for seven years. Once over the rocky perimeter the carpet of tree mallow took over. The vegetation squeaked as I walked across it towards the ruins. The men grew crops here, their neglected field walls hid away under the growth of heather and bracken. It was a small oasis, the green land being protected from the hungry sea by a fortress of granite coast. I sat on top of one of the bare stone walls, dangling my feet and looking down inside the building. It had a story, but it could not speak: the long years had rendered it silent. Soon the archaeologists would be measuring it up, taking its photograph and making notes; then the autopsy would start. I could hear them coming towards me, squeaking across the vegetation. I jumped down and made my way to the northern coast.

Across another thirty foot of tree mallow and I was back on the rocky shore. This time the ruins were made of metal and wood. Great lumps of ship's hull and twisted forms of iron, washed up and left on the wayside. Two miles away the last bastion of England, the Bishop Rock Lighthouse, stood in a golden path of sun-lit sea.

To climb the summit of a small island is almost irresistible and Rosevear was no exception. An island has only got one highest point and Rosevear's doesn't quite manage to muster up fifty feet, but even so, it was the top, and I wanted to go. The archaeologists were still busily eying up the stone remains so I headed west. The view from the top of the stone summit was total. To the east lay Scilly and thirty five miles away, Land's End could only be guessed at. To the west, a few remainders of the Western Rocks, the Bishop Rock Lighthouse and three thousand miles of Atlantic Ocean. To the south-west lay the brooding lump of the Gilstone, taker of two thousand lives and the British navy's flagship, the HMS Association. A mile to the west a small wave broke, marking the presence of the Retarrier Ledges. In 1875, the SS Schiller struck the ledges and went down, taking with her 335 lives.

I wondered how we were doing for time. Down by the ruins the archaeologists were still working. I made my way back down the summit and rejoined them. We had five minutes left. Alec was rowing back to the landing place when one of the workers came over to me. "John, I think there is something wrong with this camera, it doesn't feel right." He was right, the film hadn't taken up onto the spool. I put it right and he hurriedly went back to the ruins. I thought that for my last five minutes, which was probably more like four minutes by now, I would skate over to the east coast. I never made it. On my way I came across a lesser black backed gull. It was alive but its days were numbered. It had a broken wing and was hopping about amongst the bracken and rocks. I looked across to the roofless building and then along to the wreckage strewn coast. It was time to go.

Back on the Gloria we broke out the food and opened the flasks of coffee. My thoughts wondered as the archaeologists compared notes. The ruins, the wrecked ships and the seagull were on my mind. Sandwiched between the mellowing sea and sky, caressed by the sun's orange light lay the world's travesty. What can a person do except think about Rosevear?

Alec fired the engine back to life. We tossed our coffee dregs overboard and resealed our flasks. "Let's go somewhere," somebody said. The sun had dropped below the eye of the lighthouse. Strands of cloud were building up. We accepted the offer of a glorious sunset and headed off towards the Bishop Rock. We passed the Retarrier Ledges at a respectful distance, their deadly lines only just above sea level. The ragings of the engine kept our party silent, each of us with our own thoughts. The delicate clouds were glowing, the waves were sympathetic. Fat and smouldering, the sun drowned. We reached the Bishop with our heads cocked. Alec turned off the engine. The 'Gloria' rolled gently.

From the Bishop's head, like a crown of thorns, the nets of the helicopter pad fanned out. We drank mugs of steaming coffee and ate chunks of bread and cheese. When we had finished we put on our jumpers and Alec started the engine. The keepers stepped out onto the platform, we waved good-bye to them and headed off into the evening, back to St Mary's. Back home.

Introduction to Photographs

I am attracted to islands which have had at least some history of human habitation. When Man builds his dwellings, fashions his graves, factories and cars, there must come a point when they are left to ruin and decay. The iron from an old tractor, once prized from the land and later abandoned by Man, is left to rejoin its natural state along with the rocks and soil of the surrounding terrain. The overgrown remains of an abandoned granite dwelling look as natural as the clouds in the sky. The human structure returns to nature.

This brief interruption in the 'life' of this natural material is an injection of human exploitation, a sort of National Service after which it carries on with its normal existence, yet carrying the scars and encumbrances of human interference. These remains are of high interest to me: farm machinery, no longer used by humans, covered in undergrowth or lying amongst autumn leaves in a forest corner; abandoned cars, red with rust, resting after 1,500,000 miles. Nature cannot be overcome. The encroachment of animal life into the advanced industrial estates of Man never ceases. I like to document people working with nature, as if they were riding on the crest of a fifty foot wave. Humans try so hard to go against the forces of nature and fail so miserably, not only harming themselves but the environment they live in. To live on an island is to realise the tangibility of natural forces. An islander co-operates much more with the surroundings, purely out of necessity.

There is a slot in the natural world for the human race but not content, humanity has seeped out like corrosive battery acid to create an unhealthy friction, forever trying to live on top of or outside the natural world instead of living and co-operating with it.

Plate 2

Plate 3

Plate 4

Plate 5

Plate 6

Plate 7

Plate 8

Plate 9

Plate 10

Plate 11

Plate 12

Plate 13

Plate 14

Plate 15

Plate 16

Plate 17

Plate 18

Plate 19

Plate 20

Plate 21

Plate 22

Plate 23

Plate 24

Plate 25

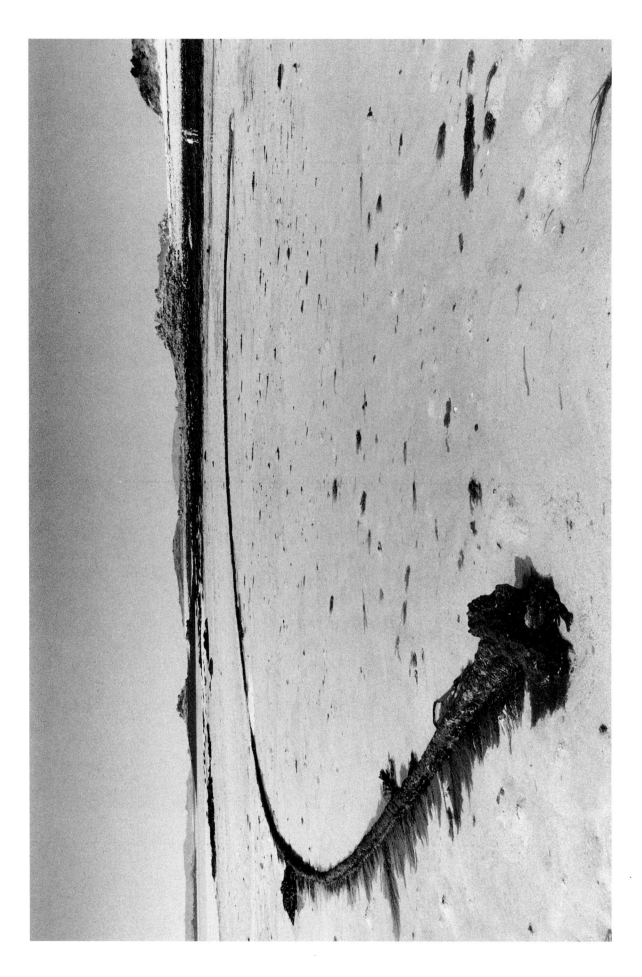

Plate 26

Plate 27

Plate 28

Plate 29

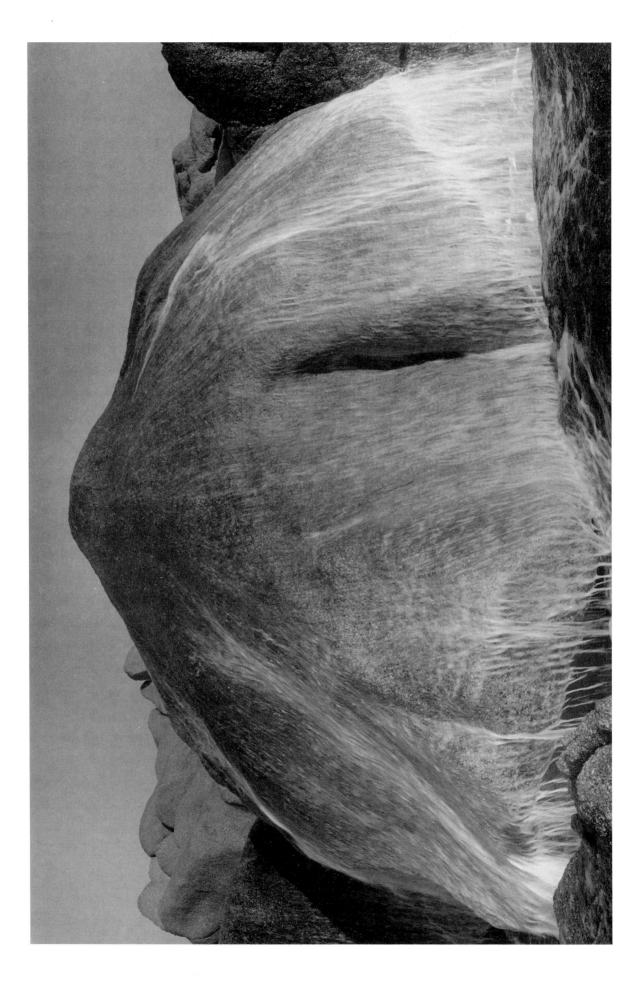

Plate 30

Plate 31

Plate 32

Plate 33

Plate 34

Plate 35

Plate 36

Plate 37

Plate 38

Plate 39

Plate 40

Plate 41

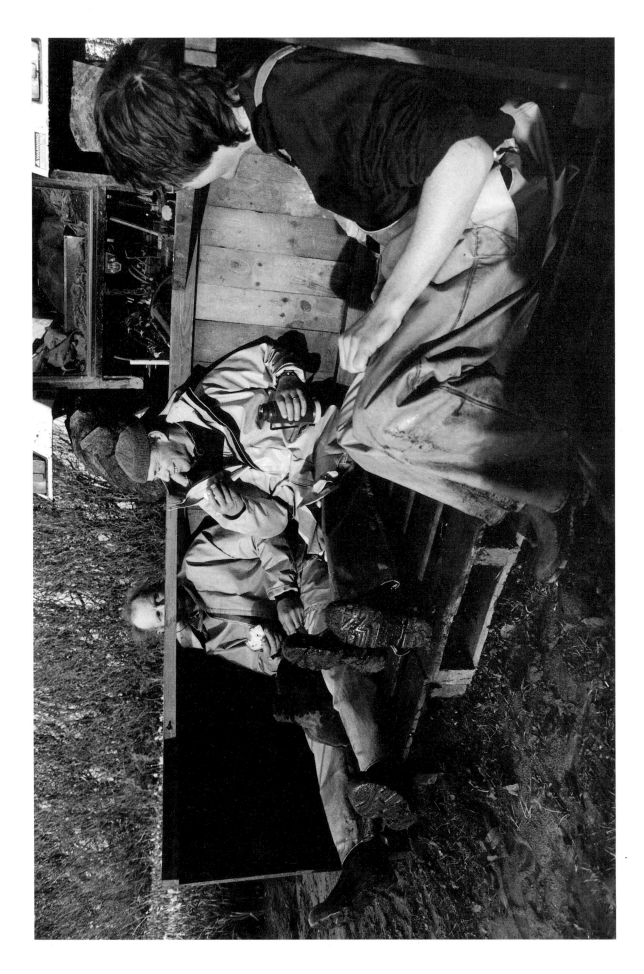

Plate 42

Plate 43

Plate 44

Plate 45

Plate 46

Plate 47

Plate 48

Plate 49

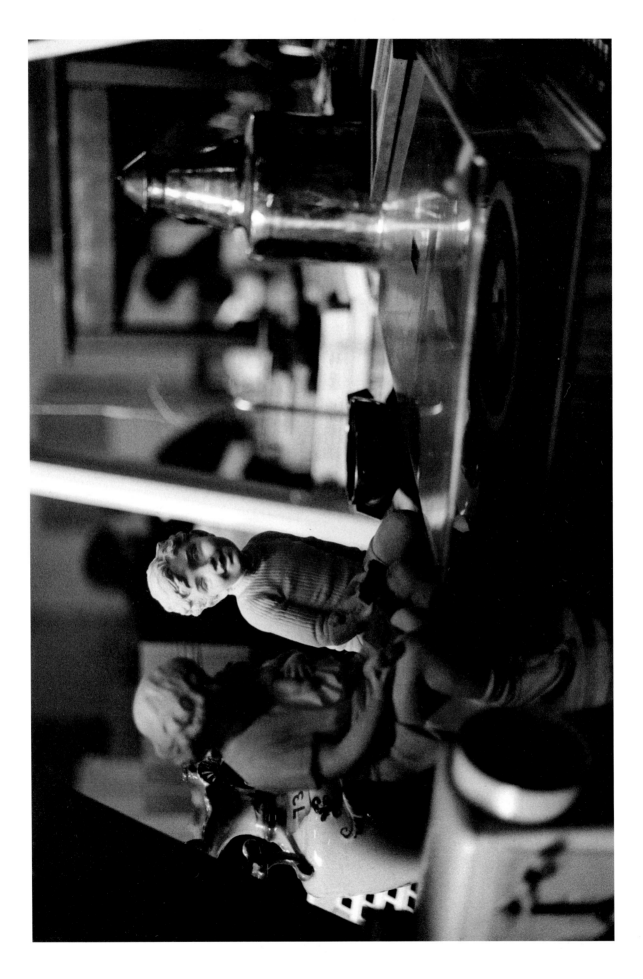

Plate 50

Plate 51

Plate 52

Plate 53

Plate 54

Plate 55

Plate 56

Plate 57

Plate 58

Plate 59

Plate 60

Plate 61

Plate 62

Plate 63

Plate 64

Plate 65

Plate 66

Plate 67

Plate 68

Plate 69

Plate 70

Plate 71

Plate 72

Plate 73

Plate 74

Plate 75

Plate 76

Plate 77

Plate 78

Plate 79

Plate 80

These winds of change, physical and
social, come and go. The stones still stand.
They have seen it all before. The sea
still lashes, the birds still cry and the
weather continues with its inexhaustible
battery of magic tricks and practical jokes.
This, then, is the real Scilly.

I would like to thank the following people who helped
in various ways to produce the finished book:

Clive, Gail, Daphne, Alun, Barbara, George and
Mervion who read through the typescript and Gordon
who also took the photograph of me.

Jacky, who relentlessly keyed in the text onto disk and
battled with me into the early hours with the final
editing, turning my text into readable English.

Roy for the wonderful preface.

Jeanette, Andy and Cathy of the Cornwall
Archaeological Unit and Alec the Boatman.

Special thanks to Jef, Jools and Adrian from 41 Design
who proved invaluable and did more than just design
Islands Apart.

Signed photographs
available from
Wruff Photography,
Porthloo, St Mary's,
Isles of Scilly.

Index to Photographs